Essential Skills for Growing Old with Grace

A Sampler of Wit, Wisdom, & Observations

AGING WITH FINESSE, BOOK 3

Mary L. Flett, PhD

Five Pillars of Aging Press

Sonoma, California

D1261064

Published in the United States by:

Five Pillars of Aging Press	Five Pillars of Aging Press
P.O. Box 134	157 Temelec Circle
El Verano, CA 95433	Sonoma, CA 95476

https://fivepillarsofaging.com

Five Pillars of Aging Press First Edition, 2021
First Printing
Cover Design: Jessica Reed

Book Layout © 2017 BookDesignTemplates.com

Essential Skills for Growing Old with Grace. -- 1st ed.
ISBN: 978-1-7342395-7-7

This book is dedicated Rebecca Latimer, Alex Flett, Hillevi Ruumet, Arthur Hastings, Jill Mellick, Robert Frager, and my husband, Hank Parker, each of whom provided me with essential skills necessary to age better and age well. From them, through them, and now in me and through me, this legacy continues.

We know now that this life is whole. The first part was good, so good. Why would be doubt for a moment that this half will be anything less?

Now the Mystery is about to reveal itself. Now the time is complete. Now it is finished. Now it is only beginning.

—Joan Chittister

Contents

Preface

I STARTED WRITING A WEEKLY BLOG in November, 2017 for the Center for Aging and Values. This was my opportunity to explore issues that have essential importance to me as an aging adult and, at that time, to my patients. Since then, I have published a blog every Sunday including several guest blogs and a couple of reprints of blogs I thought had "legs".

In 2020, faced with the consequences of COVID, I decided to pull my blogs together and publish them in book format. This journey has resulted in the Aging with Finesse series, of which this is the third book. Contents differ slightly from the original postings (and are much improved) due of the excellent editorial eye of Cathy Cambron.

This book contains information that is more grounded in "how-tos" than the previous two yet doesn't quite fit into a do-it-yourself category. As in the other two, in this book I draw on examples from my own family as well as the collective shared stories from friends, mentors, and patients over the years.

Essential skills are attitudes that help us navigate the shoals and rapids that we encounter with increasing frequency as we age. Learning new things, being compassionate with ourselves and others, knowing what "good enough" means, and standing in our power turn out to be fundamental to creating and maintaining a high quality of life.

It is my belief that these skill sets have less to do with putting aside sufficient money for retirement and more to do with ensuring that we are capable of taking steps necessary to be present to whatever is happening in our life and to make the most of it.

Acknowledgments

THIS SERIES OF BOOKS WOULD not have come to see the light of day without the support and encouragement of Hillevi Ruumet, who lent me her eagle eye for proofreading and who spent countless hours in conversation with me pondering purpose and meaning. She continues to add value and meaning to my life.

I also have deep gratitude for the support of Ruth Schwartz and her far-reaching network of experts who helped me launch these words into the world of self-publishing.

Finally, I thank the core readers of my blog, who over the past four years have provided me with validation and inspiration to share my observations and insights on valuing ourselves as we grow older.

FIXING OURSELVES

Originally published December 6, 2020

THE *NEW YORK TIMES* RAN a piece called "How to Fix America" last week. The editor, Andrew Ross Sorkin, asked "experts" what one simple thing could be done to make our nation better. Responses came from economic experts, banking experts, anthropologists, high-tech gurus, education specialists, environmental entrepreneurs, politicians—even a cop! But nowhere in this list of experts were philosophers, religious or spiritual advisers, or (as far as I could tell) wise elders. The failure to include these is an oversight.

Accepting Ourselves First

I have had several careers in my lifetime, all of which involved identifying problems, exploring solutions, and then implementing strategies to change circumstances for the better. I think I can speak as an "expert" (and am happy to share my bona fides, if you wish) and offer this response to the challenge posed by the *New York Times* editor: we need to fix ourselves before we fix anything else.

Do Nothing

Let me be specific. Making our nation better requires that we each be responsible for ourselves and the impact our words, behaviors and choices have on others. As a psychologist, I spent countless hours exploring these very elements with people who experienced differing degrees of guilt, elation, and remorse in coming to terms with themselves. While I was able to offer different approaches to confront these dilemmas, the ultimate solution was not about fixing, but about accepting.

Making our nation better requires that we accept the fact that we have been given incredible opportunities and have squandered too many, ignored quite a few, and done some things worthy of praise and repetition. Making our nation better requires that we accept our failures and—instead of forging ahead and just creating new problems—that we pause, reflect, and consider whether to proceed at all. Making our nation better requires that, for the moment at least, we do nothing.

This is a lesson understood by those of us living with bodies that are breaking down, minds that wander in labyrinths of memories while trying to remember names, and metabolisms that are slower and less efficient. This is a lesson in understanding the long-term benefits of resisting immediate gratification. This is a lesson teaching us that if we had paused rather than acted impulsively in our youth, we would have the luxury of different choices now. But you don't learn these lessons until you get to be a certain age.

Wisdom Sourcing

As elders, we need to speak up! We offer evidence that the present moment is just one in a chain of moments that stretches forward and backward and merely holds our attention for now. We are the living evidence that we can survive this present and make a future. We must take advantage of those among us who daily share their wisdom with others. Instead of waiting around to be asked, we need to step into the breach and offer our services.

A favorite book that I return to over and over is titled *What Are Old People For?* How do you answer that question? In these most extraordinary of times, what is your function? What are you contributing? How are you engaging with life? I suggest to you that you are incredibly valuable and that you are in great demand.

Keep Your Eyes on the Horizon

We are at a critical juncture in the history of our nation. While the pull is to stay focused on the immediate future, it is up to those of us who have experienced difficult times to keep our eyes on the horizon and remind those who have not yet developed the skills to tolerate discomfort and uncertainty that we can and will make it through this moment.

We are waking now, hungover from a memorable binge of good times (admittedly not for all), excess and indulgence in online purchase of goods and consumption of ideas, and a promise of a brighter future. All along there have been voices telling us there would be consequences. We are just beginning to come to terms with our withdrawal and will need steady hands to guide us through the coming days, when the consequences of our actions are no longer able to be ignored. There are those among us, me included, who welcome this accounting.

What Is Your Role?

I clearly see what my role is as a wise elder. I am charged with keeping alive the legacy of the past. Not idealizing it; not romanticizing it. Taking from the past the crucial elements that are necessary for our survival and ensuring that these are passed on to the next generation. Acting from hard-won knowledge that holding on to resentments only makes the pain worse. Holding the line and keeping those who would do harm to the community in check. Seeing that they are disciplined not out of revenge, but in the spirit of reconciliation. Creating community. Ensuring that all members within it are cared for. Guaranteeing that there is enough for all by fostering gratitude, not greed. Providing an example of what can be—by being it.

Earlier this year I attended a rally organized by youth in my community in response to the George Floyd murder. I was brought to tears as they shared their pain arising from feeling marginalized because of their age, made invisible and silenced because of the color of their skin, their gendered lives, and their economic status. What struck me is that this pain is also experienced by many older adults. I was reminded of my own coming-of-age adventures during the 1970s, protesting the war in Vietnam, marching for civil rights, and demanding justice for all. My lesson here is that in the interim, the suffering has not diminished, but my ability to be compassionate with myself and others has increased. And to be compassionate in that way is the most valuable advice I can offer.

If You Have the Means

What is one thing that you can do to fix our nation? Be a better you. If you have the means to offer relief to others, then do so, whether it be by sending money to charity or by saying something kind to someone. If you have the means to provide shelter, food, and safety, then do so and inspire others to join you in that effort. If you have the means to influence others in taking steps to be healthy, then do so, knowing your efforts are making a difference in all our lives. If you have the means to reduce worry in others, then do so by wearing a mask, staying home, and reaching out to family and friends to assure them they are loved and valued by you. If you have the means to pray, then do so, and pray for all those who are lost or in need of support, direction, and comfort. If you have the means to bring joy or laughter or delight to others, then do so freely and energetically.

And if you think you don't have the means to do anything, then just love yourself. Sometimes it is in pausing and doing nothing that the greatest transformation happens.

INSPIRATION

Originally published February 2, 2020

I SPENT THIS AFTERNOON IN the company of a group of incredibly creative women. This is not an unusual experience for me, and for that I am very grateful. Women seem to have a natural affinity for collaboration and connection that results in everybody experiencing something new about themselves. Earlier, I had started my blog in a very distressed and dark place, but because of my participation in a wonderfully connected and creative group process, I was lifted from that place and transported to a place of hope and inspiration.

We are living in dark times, but we do not need to spend all our time in darkness. There are moments that bring joy and relief and contentment and peace. Each of these temporary states of being can provide a moment of release from a dominant story line of doom. All the best writers have found ways to balance the doom and darkness with the light. I wish all of us could attend a master class where we would learn the skill of constructing such balanced storytelling.

Fairy Tales

I was raised on fairy tales. These were fantasies that ended in reassuring ways, with evil always overcome by goodness. While there were dark (very dark) characters who did things that were unacceptable, good always seemed to win out, and a lesson was offered that, if learned, would keep me safe, or at least aware of the harm that would befall me if I did not heed the warning. Sometimes I wonder whether these lessons were valuable, or whether I was somehow being set up for a fall.

Our current political environment seems to demand that we set aside our values and beliefs and instead rely on how spinmeisters and others interpret our shared reality and make meaning of what is happening. We seem to be invited to make our way into the dark forest, following only the bread crumbs left behind by strangers or the promise of food and shelter from a disguised being. We are not paying attention to our senses and our intuition. Instead, we have abdicated our own knowledge and have decided that others know better or have more awareness of what is going on.

Sharing Our Heart's Desire

While our inner vision may be clear, it is fragile and easily tarnished. Our heart's desire is frequently different from what we share with others—partly because we fear judgment and ridicule, but more often because we have little faith that we are deserving of what we truly want. In asking for our heart's desire, we defend against the loss we anticipate instead of expecting the joy of receiving a blessing. Oh, how very different our lives would be if that were the reality.

It takes courage to envision a life in which our heart's desire is met. It takes boldness to clearly see ourselves having the love we are worthy of having, the home we are meant to occupy, the job we are destined to do, and the kind of life that we are capable of living. For many, it is selfish to think of these things. For others, it is bad juju that will jinx the outcome.

What if we lived in a state of mind in which our dreams were achievable? What if we spent the time to focus on what we really, truly wanted, knowing that all that was required was to visualize and manifest? That idea might be so overwhelming that some would cower and fall away from the vision. Or it might inspire us to see a world of our own making.

A Certain Magical Power

In my experience, thoughts are just thoughts. But when those thoughts have energy, passion, vision, and commitment to action behind them, there is a certain magical power that seems to coalesce. Manifesting our dreams is not easy. It requires effort to be clear about what we want and to not doubt our worth in claiming our dreams.

Clarity and intention seem to produce results regardless of the moral weight of the dream. This is a difficult truth to accept. This truth seems to have little to do with right or wrong. So the debate about worthiness is often a short one.

Whatever your dreams, I hope you are willing to commit to making them a reality. It takes nothing to dream a dream. It takes effort and commitment to turn that dream into reality.

The only way I know how to change the world is to combine your dream with commitment these efforts.

LOOKING LEFT AND RIGHT

Originally published January 28, 2018

LOOKING TO THE RIGHT AND the left before you cross the street was a lesson I learned early in my life. For some reason, it has stuck with me not so much for its safety value, but for its value in expanding my peripheral vision. I wish more people would look to the left and the right before they do anything.

One of the challenges of growing old in a culture that demands we produce something all the time is that we lose sight of those peripheral jewels. In our goal to live longer and longer we miss out on the expansiveness of what has accompanied us on our journey.

Looking to the left, maybe you caught a glimpse of yourself wearing bell-bottoms or a beard and can laugh at what you used to think was fashionable. Looking to the right, maybe you have found that music, books, poetry, and dance evoke all your emotions and spark cascading memories that cross over decades. Now you seek out these art forms because they make you feel alive.

Challenging Habitual Ways of Thinking

In asking you to look to your left and right, I invite you to affirmatively challenge what might have become your habitual way of thinking and behaving. We have tasked the artist with the job of paying attention to the peripheral for us. I am inviting you, dear reader, to take up this task as the artisan of your life.

To do so requires several changes in your thinking, one or two changes in your doing, and lastly one single change in your being. To wit: You are required to be willing. Willingness is the incubator of creation. Willingness is the repository of action. Willingness is the root bed of change.

Willingness v. Willfulness

I am not talking about willfulness. For most of us willfulness is, unfortunately, an intimate familiar. It is the place where we say "I have to have it my way!" and "Unless it is as I expect, it is not worth it!" Willfulness is the exclamatory stance in the face of true awareness. Willfulness is crossing the freeway while tweeting.

Willingness, on the other hand, is the openly brazen acceptance of what is and the faith (or perhaps grace) to not be attached to outcome. Attachment to willfulness brings with it fear and mistrust, anxiety and worries—all those uncomfortable and unwelcome feelings that, ironically, will melt away if you are just willing to stay with the experience.

Willingness comes as a preloaded app in our infant selves. It is the mercurial change of emotions based on sensory information—one minute a gleeful burp, the next a tearful response to loud noise. Willingness is the joy of playing endless games of peek-a-boo and the soothing calmness of being rocked to sleep with a lullaby.

What happens as we age, however, is that our willingness is tempered through disappointment, unmet expectations, criticism, and loss. These events work on our willingness like the buildup of plaque on teeth. At some point, most likely without any awareness at all, we find ourselves focused on one or two things, acquiring regret and investing in a future that is filled with anticipatory pain.

Here is where the other actions I noted earlier become essential. Change your thinking and your ways of doing things, and you can rediscover willingness.

Changing Your Thinking

How do you change your thinking? The very first step is to be aware of the thought itself. Ironically, people who are very anxious and worried are already skilled at this recognition. They can identify every mote of terror, catastrophe, and pain in excruciating detail. The rest of us may experience a "thought" only occasionally or as part of yoga, meditation, or other forms of mindfulness.

The second step in changing your thinking is to let go of the thought instead of holding on to it.

Many metaphors exist for this step—watching clouds in the sky (each cloud is a thought), watching leaves on a river as they float by—but my favorite is looking for space between railroad cars as they make their way, clickety-clack, across the rails. The slower the train is going, the easier it is to see the space!

The next step is to change what you are doing. We are creatures of habit, sometimes to the detriment of our overall health and well-being. For example, once we find a food we like, we may continue to choose it over other types rather than try something new. Or we may take the same route to a location instead of trying the road less taken. Or we may find ourselves listening to rhetoric of people we "like" rather than making an effort to understand people we "disagree with" because the former is easier. These actions need to be systematically challenged in order to keep our brain active and flexible.

Start Small

You don't need to start with the big things. You can actually make small changes that will have a big effect. One example is to brush your teeth with your "other" hand. Another is to sleep on a different side of your bed. Still another is to challenge yourself to eat something new or listen to a different type of music. Results will be swift and most informative. Pay attention to how irritated or resistant to doing these things you are; that will tell you how wedded you have become to doing things your way.

So what are you willing to do that will open your experience and widen the focus of your life? What will you see when you look left and then right before you cross the street?

The Roman philosopher Seneca reminds us: "Yet the greatest waste of life lies in postponement: it robs us of each day in turn and snatches away the present by promising the future. The greatest impediment to living is expectancy, which relies on tomorrow and wastes today. You map out what is in fortune's hand but let slip what's in your own hand. What are you aiming at? What's your goal? All that's to come, lies in uncertainty: live right now."

HAVING HARD CONVERSATIONS:

PART I

Originally published December 3, 2017

SOME THINGS ARE AWKWARD TO talk about (like having food stuck in your teeth). Some things are uncomfortable to talk about (like sex). Some things nobody wants to talk about at all. Hard conversations are the ones you know will be difficult to start, much less get through, without feeling angry, uncomfortable, hurt, or afraid—or for that matter, any other negatively charged emotion. Yet, these are conversations that are most needed, precisely because they are hard.

One of these is what you want to do about dying.

The Best Laid Plans

Almost to a person, folks I know are "planning" on dying at home. Yet very few of them have taken the necessary steps to make sure they can. Here's what I mean. For you to die at home in your bed, you should have already discussed and completed the following steps:

- Completed a durable power of attorney for health care
- Funded and executed a will or trust
- Completed the "physician orders for life-sustaining treatment" (POLST) form
- Interviewed, vetted, and hired or contracted with caregivers willing to care for you at home
- Obtained buy-in from primary care, spouse, children, partners, friends
- Created written instructions about your wishes

The first two steps require you to at least consult with an attorney or paralegal who knows and understands advanced care planning in your state. The third step requires that you have a conversation with your primary care provider. Yes, it is going to cost you some money—probably less than that new iPhone. The last three steps require that you have hard conversations with your loved ones. We'll go over these in Part II.

Durable Power of Attorney for Health Care (aka Advanced Care Directive)

The durable power of attorney for health care (DPA-HC) is a legal document that gives decision-making power to someone else when and if you can't or don't want to make these decisions yourself. This person will make decisions on your behalf using the guidelines you have identified. The key here is that the decisions are being made on your behalf by someone you have chosen.

I encourage you to really think this choice through. Maybe you think your son or daughter is the best one to make these decisions because s/he is your child. But does s/he have the skill set to remain strong and objective while being bombarded with questions from nurses, doctors, and social workers requiring decisions that may have consequences like whether you will be placed in a nursing home for the next five years on a respirator and feeding tube?

Does s/he have a good understanding of what you want because you have had many heart-to-heart conversations about these decisions? Are there others who might have a different point of view who would try to influence or change your child's mind?

Depending on your answers, you may decide that your child is not the best person to have make these decisions. Then you will need to find someone who will.

POLST

In the past ten years, the United States has seen a shift in end-of-life decision-making. One initiative that has gained traction across the country is the POLST. Unlike a durable power of attorney for health care, this is a medical order that gives instructions to emergency response personnel on what you want to have happen in the event of a medical emergency. (Google POLST programs in your state to see what is going on locally.)

Because the POLST is a medical order, emergency personnel won't automatically start life-saving interventions if you or someone else calls 911. If you are in a hospital or nursing home, the POLST will act as standing orders regarding how to proceed as your dying process continues.

What you need is sort of a belt-and-suspenders thing. You want both the DPA-HC and a POLST to ensure your intentions are carried out.

Wills and Trusts

The POLST and the DPA-HC will cover your choices up until the time you die. After your death, your wishes are managed using a will, a trust, or both. These legal documents are designed to make sure your assets (house, bank accounts, and land) are managed and distributed the way you desire. These documents are used to handle the tedious details of death (paying off debts, closing bank accounts, selling property) that you no longer can do because you are dead.

My Story

I am especially passionate about folks having these conversations because I learned the hard way what happens when there are no clear guidelines in place and when all parties aren't on board. My husband and I had discussed what we wanted to happen if either of us got sick. He had diabetes and was experiencing a decline in his overall health. He was on the verge of going on dialysis when he had an episode of kidney failure. He had clearly stated to me that he did not want any extraordinary measures—just comfort care—and so had signed a do-not-resuscitate order (DNR). This was on file with the hospital.

I called 911. We went to the emergency room. The ER doc said, "You have a DNR, how do you want us to proceed?" My husband, still fully conscious and frightened by the reality of what was going on, said, "Revoke the DNR!"

He was admitted to the hospital with total kidney failure. While in the hospital, he acquired an infection that rapidly caused him to go from worse to being on death's door. He became septic and was no longer able to make decisions for himself.

We had him transferred to another hospital where he spent two weeks in the intensive care unit. He was transitioned from ICU to a cardiac care floor, where he was put on dialysis. He never recovered his ability to made decisions and wavered between being able to recognize his children and me and being totally out of it.

His children and I had never shared a close relationship, and my husband had not had the hard conversation with them, so we were literally on opposite sides of the bed trying to decide what would be best. In spite of knowing what he wanted, we were unable to see those wishes carried out.

Three weeks after being admitted to the second hospital, my husband died of heart failure. The doctor called me and said, "We did everything we could. We did CPR for forty-five minutes but could not bring him back." The irony is that in the many conversations my husband and I had had about what kind of care he wanted, he was very clear that he did not want CPR.

Since his death I have gone over what I could have, should have, and would have done differently. I am making sure that I have the hard conversations with those whom I am asking to make the journey with me so that I can ensure that my wishes are clearly understood and carried out.

HAVING HARD CONVERSATIONS:

PART II

Originally published December 10, 2017

LAST WEEK I WROTE ABOUT the medical and legal side of dying the way you want to (Part I). Today we'll look at getting buy-in from the people who will carry out your wishes. There are three broad areas that need to be addressed:

- Finding and hiring caregivers willing to care for you at home
- Obtaining buy-in from primary care, spouse, children, partners, friends
- Creating written instructions for your wishes

Now, how do you have the hard conversations about these steps? The University of California, San Francisco and the Veteran's Administration have developed a wonderful online tool to walk you through the questions that are essential in having this hard conversation. Known as "PREPARE for Your Care," this self-paced program will help you identify all your wishes about being cared for: who, what, where, when, and how. Do follow the link and work your way through this very thorough process.

Decision-Making Qualities

What are the qualities you want in someone who will make decisions for you? Identifying qualities, such as being detail-oriented or having experience, instead of focusing on duties or tasks usually ends up with you finding a better candidate. For example, handing me a list of tasks you want done (pay bills, water plants) is going to work only if I am good with numbers or care about gardening.

This is a more challenging conversation and will take a while, but it is definitely worth the effort. Here is a partial list; see which qualities you think are important.

The person(s) making decisions for me should be:

Careful	Available
Systematic	Logical
Thorough	Opinionated
Even-tempered	Emotional
Thoughtful	Objective
Caring	Punctual
Passionate	Responsible
Able and willing to take reasonable risks on my behalf	

Think about which of these qualities appeal to you and why you think they would ensure that you get the care you want and need. Feel free to add or remove qualities. This is about *you!*

Who Will Make the Decision?

Once you have identified the qualities that are important to you, you will need to identify people who have some or all of those qualities.

This is one of those hard conversations. What if the best choice isn't a family member? Maybe your son or daughter is the apple of your eye, but s/he doesn't have the qualities to make decisions for you? Same goes for siblings, spouses, and friends.

Here, you may need to consult with a trusted friend, therapist, spiritual counselor, or medical professional to work through the uncomfortable feelings and come up with a plan that meets *your* needs. Therapists, counselors, and medical professionals can help facilitate these conversations and may serve as a welcome authority that will take the pressure off you.

Who Wants to Talk about This?

Many of us are not very skilled at talking about death and dying. Perhaps your loved ones don't want to have the conversation at all. Avoidance of this topic is understandable. And yet it is such an important conversation to have. Expect it to be uncomfortable and awkward. You can still have this talk!

In my experience, many people are afraid of hurting someone's feelings. This fear just doesn't make sense! I have heard too many stories in which one sibling is angry at another because s/he didn't do what Mom or Dad wanted. Or a spouse (especially if it is a second marriage) has different ideas about what is needed from the kids. Or even, in situations in which there are no close relatives, a distant cousin is called on to make decisions without really knowing the person the cousin is now responsible for. This is not the time to be doing family therapy.

What about Caregivers?

More and more boomers are experiencing an interesting dilemma: those whom we reasonably expect to care for us (partners, spouses, children) may be experiencing their own health challenges and may not be able to offer help. Did you know that the majority of caregiving in the United States is provided by family members—typically spouses?

Based on what many of my patients have experienced, finding qualified care is daunting. There are a couple of reasons. One is that most of us are not skilled at the hiring process: interviewing, checking references, figuring out how much to pay and following up. Another is that there aren't that many caregivers to choose from. So it pays to do some research ahead of time. AARP has a wonderful website that will help you determine what you need.

Here's a brief checklist:

- Ask friends about caregivers they have used and what they experienced.
- Call your local Council on Aging and ask about a referral list.
- Understand your legal obligations (such as taxes and insurance).
- If you hire an individual who does not work for an agency (known as an independent contractor), make sure you are not at risk for having to pay for unemployment insurance or disability insurance if the person is injured while working for you.
- Know the going rate for services in your area and the laws about minimum wage.
- Understand how much caregiving will cost and how payment is to be made. Negotiate if you can.

Written Instructions for Others

Knowing what you or your loved one needs so you can specifically ask the potential caregiver whether s/he is ready, willing, and able to take care of those needs is essential. Many family members just "know" what is needed. But letting a "stranger" into that implicit web of understanding can be a challenge.

For example, many people have their medications stored outside of the pill bottles they came in. They have patterns and habits of taking their meds, or bathing, or making meals that seem obvious to them but may be confusing or illogical to someone outside of the family. You may eat only certain foods at certain times. You may prefer to watch sports, movies, or a shopping network. Most important, you may have fourteen remotes that each need to be used in a certain order so that you can watch that movie!

Most caregivers are not qualified mind readers. (For that matter, most spouses aren't either!) It can be an eye-opening assignment to identify each of your unique preferences and habits. No sense in causing undue stress and tension when you are not at your best. So taking care of this task ahead of time is essential.

Five Steps

1. It is vital that you have these hard conversations before things start to go south.
2. Acknowledge that these conversations are hard and have them more than once.
3. Use the resources of trusted advisers and others who have gone through similar experiences.
4. Learn what is involved in hiring a caregiver if you aren't going to be the one who provides the care.
5. Take some time to write down what is unique and special about you and your loved ones so that if someone from outside your network takes care of you, he or she can easily fit in.

A little planning ahead of time can make a big difference for all.

DEALING WITH LOSS

Originally published August 12, 2018

LOSS IS HARD AT ANY age, and as we grow older the frequency of our losses increases. But just what is "loss"? I like to think of it as the absence of the familiar.

Some losses are expected. By the time we reach our mid-sixties, many of us have lost a parent. While this is an unwelcome event, it is not unexpected. Depending on the kind of relationship you had with your deceased parent, his or her absence may affect you in a variety of ways, including grief, sadness, emptiness, or perhaps even gratitude.

Loss of a Sibling or Peer

When we lose a sibling or peer, we lose a shared history and collective memory of our childhood. Loss of a sibling can be devastating. Siblings are unique witnesses who can validate your memory and experience of growing up. While the details may differ, there is still comfort in recalling shared life.

Not all of us have siblings. I am an only child, and in many ways, my classmates provide me with the same contemporaneous accounting of my life that siblings do. I remember attending my fortieth high school reunion and being astonished at how many of my classmates had died in their thirties and forties. Their deaths were a shock to me because these classmates continued to be vibrantly alive in my memory, albeit frozen in time. Their deaths held up that mirror of certainty that I too, will die.

Unexpected Losses

Other losses are unexpected. These range from loss of a child to loss of homes and heirlooms from natural and manmade disasters. These unexpected losses carry with them the burden of unfulfilled futures or legacies that can no longer be passed down in physical form.

Loss is unique in that no matter how we imagine it, the actual experience is always different. We may find ourselves "rehearsing" the death of parents, pets, friends, or others, but it is not until we learn of the actual event that our world is irrevocably changed. Until that moment, there is some magical thinking that leads us to believe that such a thing would never happen to us or that it would happen as we planned it.

Consequences of Loss

Loss has emotional, physical, and psychological consequences, as well as bringing changes in economic status and role responsibilities. Emotional consequences range from shutting down completely to experiencing increased anxiety, tearfulness, and guilt.

Thoughts of not wanting to live or being unable to go on with life are common and very frightening. Physical consequences include increased blood pressure, possible rapid weight gain or weight loss, sleep interruptions, and increased aches and pains. People often turn to drugs or alcohol to manage their emotional pain. Psychological consequences range from questioning the meaning of life to finding new purpose, as well as recommitting to changing things or possibly losing faith in God.

Changes in status and role are common and frequently impact how a person navigates life after a loss. Those who have lost homes to fire, floods, tornadoes, and hurricanes may not have sufficient money to rebuild or start over. Work may no longer be available, so jobs must be sought elsewhere, resulting in unplanned relocations. Older children who lose parents may need to take over parenting roles for siblings or provide care for the remaining parent.

Coping with Loss

So how do we cope with loss? Every individual has his or her own experience. But we can generalize and put these experiences into six broad categories: replace, retreat, resolve, restore, reconnect, and reengage.

"Replace" is the action often suggested to someone who has lost something precious. We see and hear this suggestion in interviews with folks who lose property and mementos in natural disasters. We use this idea to console a child after a pet dies. Forty years ago, replacement was a standard recommendation for women who lost children in childbirth or infancy: "Just have another baby."

While well meant, if replacement is sought too soon in the grieving process, people may find themselves smiling on the outside and experiencing emptiness and guilt on the inside. It may seem instinctual to make such a suggestion, but when looked at closely, it probably arises more from secretly feeling relief that the loss didn't happen to us. Besides, there really is nothing that can "replace" what has been lost.

Retreat

"Retreat" takes on the cloak of withdrawal from others. Behaviors that reflect this way of coping include fatigue, sleeping more, and desiring to be left alone. Retreat can also be intentional, giving the grieving person an opportunity to come to terms with their loss without the burdens of life depleting their capacity for functioning.

This is part of the "fight-flight-freeze" response that comes with experiencing trauma. A case can be made that any loss is traumatic, and unexpected loss is intensely traumatic. Many describe initial days after a loss as passing in a "fog." This is a type of self-protective dissociation that allows a person to continue to function but numbs the pain of the loss for days or months.

Resolve

"Resolve" is what is seen in an experience in which the loss itself provides a solution to a problem that seemed unsolvable. For example, death often brings family members back together again, thus resolving years of not speaking to one another. On the other hand, an adult child may be waiting for an inheritance, which resolves an economic problem.

Restore

"Restore" is an action that becomes possible once the initial shock of the loss has lessened. This strategy is often seen in people vowing to rebuild or create a new sense of community. Natural disasters that occurred in Puerto Rico, Haiti, and New Orleans suggest that many people will come together to help others get back on their feet. And similar acts of compassion are found in gatherings to which people bring "covered dishes" to show their support and concern for those who have lost a loved one. In sharing this way, both the giver and the receiver find themselves restored.

Reconnect

"Reconnect" is an activity that typically comes later in the grieving process. People may find themselves having more energy or laughing once again. The fatigue that once kept them home lifts, and desire for the company of others increases. Animals seem to have a unique way of helping with reconnecting that allow those who have experienced loss to open their hearts and risk being hurt again.

Reengage

"Reengage" for most people is something they can do after coming to terms with the absence and turning once again toward life. There is no timeline for this. Many people report that in this stage they became aware that their thoughts were no longer focused on the past but remained in the present or went more frequently to the future.

There are always bumps along the way, especially around anniversary dates (such as the loved one's death day, birthday, or anniversary). And there will always be reminders such as a song, or a smell, or a familiar place that may trigger an emotional response. But instead of being drawn down into despair, when the stage of reengaging is reached, these experiences are temporary and less intense, and eventually they may even become welcome.

We cannot avoid loss as we age. But we can open our hearts to the experience and accept support and love from those around us who want to help. If you know of someone who is grieving and needs support, check with your local hospice, faith-based community, or therapists for resources.

WEIGHTY MATTERS

Originally published August 18, 2019

THIS WEEK WENT BY FASTER than most. I was focused on a medical evaluation that happened on Wednesday. Somehow my Monday slipped by, even with appointments and a dinner party. Tuesday came and went, and was filled with purposeful activity, but I was still distracted because of the upcoming medical appointment. Finally, Wednesday arrived.

The older I get, the more medical appointments fill me with dread. I think the reason is mostly that the odds of having something wrong seem to increase with age. I walk away from most of my exams with a feeling of relief that nothing was found and I can go about my unconscious ways for a while longer.

Meeting My Goal

This time, I was focused on meeting a specific goal that would allow me to qualify for hip replacement surgery. I have been steadily losing weight now for many months. This was in preparation for meeting the body mass index (BMI) measure that was required for surgery to be done safely. The last week was the worst. I had met my weight goal but suddenly went on a binge and feared I would be told that the surgery would have to be delayed. I was consumed during the entire drive to the medical offices with arguments in my head in which I would plead for the doctors to make an exception so that I would be relieved of my pain.

I arrived at the facility, made my way in, registered, and sat nervously in the waiting room. It wasn't too long (thank God!) before I was called in for x-rays. I was given a pair of paper shorts to wear, as my slacks would have obscured the film. I actually had weighed my clothes before leaving for the appointment, just so I could say that it was their total weight that was putting me over the top. The medical assistant stepped out and let me put on my new togs, then returned and took my blood pressure. It must have been off the charts! She then asked me to get on the scale. I held my breath, closed my eyes, and gave everything over to God. When next I peeked, I literally let out a yelp of delight as the digital readout showed I had come in below the BMI requirement.

Good to Go

From that point forward, it didn't matter what the staff asked of me—I was floating. They poked and prodded, and then had me wait in a room for the surgeon. By this time I was calmer but still somehow expected to be told I would have to come back. Instead, the surgeon looked at my x-rays, told me the risks and benefits of the surgery, handed me a brochure on what to expect afterward, shook my hand and said he would see me in a few weeks. I changed back into my slacks, negotiated dates with the scheduler, and made my way back home.

That was Wednesday morning. I saw patients Wednesday afternoon, did pre-op blood work Thursday morning, met with a contractor Thursday afternoon, had dinner with friends, and drove home under a beautiful full moon. Friday, I did paperwork, saw more patients, and finally collapsed. I had been living on adrenalin for three days! Once that ran out, the pain returned.

The Potency of Pain

Truth is I have been in pain for almost seven years now. I suspect there may be many of you who are all too familiar with the exhaustion that chronic pain causes. It makes me grumpy, forgetful, distractible, and mostly very, very sad. It has a way of stealing joy out of a beautiful day and making tomorrow something to dread rather than anticipate.

Pain is so essentially human. Its very existence is required for our survival, and its persistence has led to humans trying virtually every substance and combination of substances in an attempt to find relief. In my case, I have found relief through anti-inflammatory medications, massage, and chiropractic care. Without my care providers, I would have been in worse shape, believe me.

Now, however, I can taste the freedom! In sharing my good news, many folks have told me of their experiences with this kind of surgery, and, I have to say, all have been very positive. I feel blessed to be living in an age when technology and surgical techniques are at a level that this kind of operation is done thousands of times a year, just in my area alone. I feel gratitude for having access to quality medical care and having insurance that will cover the expenses of my stay in the hospital and the physical therapy and aftercare I may need.

Gratitude

I am acutely aware that such care is not available to all—not in this country, nor around the world. I can look forward to a quick recovery and return to work with minimal problems. So many people have huge barriers or may not be able to have such life-changing surgery at all. I am among the lucky few who will be granted a reprieve from pain and an opportunity to live a longer, healthier life.

I don't take this opportunity for granted. I recognize that I have been given a chance to get my life back because of the skills of my surgeon and the availability of the intervention. I don't want to be in pain again, if I can help it. I am the one who will need to change my exercise habits, my eating, and my attitude.

PARTICIPANT /OBSERVER

Originally published October 6, 2019

I AM HAVING A CURIOUS experience that is both perplexing and a challenge to describe. I go about my activities of daily living somewhat more slowly and certainly with far more watchfulness than I did before my surgery. I pay more attention to each movement and its consequences. Prior to the surgery, pain was my primary feedback loop in determining whether I could or could not perform a given activity. That feedback loop was eliminated with the new hip, and now I am becoming reacquainted with other sensations. But it seems as if I am disconnected and, rather than being the one who is walking, talking, eating, and exercising, I am watching myself do this.

Now, I am not talking about multiple personality disorder. I am talking about something all of us have: our internal observer. Those of you familiar with meditation will instantly recognize this observer. What is different for me after surgery is what is being observed.

My Body My Self?

Any of you who have gone through major surgery may have had this experience. Before my surgery, my body was wrapped in a hermetically sealed container called skin. Yes, there were times when that container was punctured, scraped, and sometimes sliced; but, for the most part, it remained intact. Now that container has been opened and pulled apart, the old parts removed and new parts installed, and the whole thing zipped back up.

The event is clear in my mind. This intentional surgical rending of my body and exposure of my inside workings to strangers is the first and only time so far that I have experienced such vulnerability. Our bodies were not designed for these interventions. Our bodies were designed to stay hermetically sealed. That this procedure was accomplished so effortlessly and with such minor side effects is mind-boggling.

I Am Amazed

The amazement of what has happened still lingers, leaving me astonished and not quite fully reintegrated yet. The stitches are dissolved, the sutures are holding, but my ethereal self (whatever that is) is still reconnecting and adjusting to this new state of being.

I have been struck by how many of my friends and providers are "amazed" at how well I am doing. Their reactions make me pause and wonder whether I really am above the norm in my rehab or whether there is a skewed picture of what can be achieved. My friends who are physical therapists have certainly seen a broad array of people who are getting their lives back after a hip replacement. I assume that their comments on my recovery levels reflect a more accurate measure of accomplishment than people who are friends and are just saying nice things about me.

Walking

Today, for the first time in years, I put on my walking shoes. This benchmark heralds a new world of freedom for me. I have not been able to walk any distance without pain in almost seven years. I am blessed to live in a neighborhood that is conducive to meandering. I am not yet up for power walking, but strolling is within reach. I have wonderful paths to stroll on and incredible views to look at. This kind of rehabilitation heals my body and soul and helps me reconstruct how I view myself. That gap between being "disabled" and being "able-bodied" is decreasing.

For so many aging adults, myself included, there is a gap between how others see us in terms of functioning and how we see ourselves in terms of what we are able to do or have been able to do in the past. A definitive line is crossed when you go from "person" to "patient." Reclaiming that personhood is essential for rehabilitation. Putting my walking shoes on today is one way I am my reclaiming my personhood. I am no longer a hip replacement patient. I am someone who has a new hip.

Extent of Ageism

How I am perceived by others also reflects the extent of ageism in our culture. These perceptions run from those of the newly minted medical doctor or nurse, who may assume I am unfamiliar with technology and forget to look up from the screen and make eye contact with me, to the assumptions made by seasoned caregivers who think I am more limited than I actually am because they don't know me and are lumping me in with their "other" clients.

I think this ageism is also reflected in my experience of myself post-op. I have a clear image of being vigorous, healthy, and being able to work a full day, go out in the evening, and get up early the next day and start all over again. But this is not reality! I need to get extra sleep, take naps, and conserve energy wisely.

While it is essential that I keep that pre-op image alive for inspiration and motivation, it is equally essential that I attend to the new signals my body now sends me and relearn the capacities of my newly reconstructed hip.

Pushing the Boundary

I find I need to gently push myself sometimes, as I have vivid memories of both pain and functional impairment that resulted from my lifestyle choices. These included not exercising enough, being overweight, not getting enough sleep, and indulging in food that wasn't always nutritionally in my best interest.

But I am not beating myself up for these past choices—just accepting the consequences and renegotiating how I can now manage my life in a way to avoid a similar result. This shift is powerful.

Powerful Shifts

Because of this shift, the likelihood of my returning to that ideal of vigor and functioning is within the realm of possibility. Doing so will take commitment on my part. Getting there will take changing routines and attitudes. But returning to that level of functioning can (and will!) be done.

Inhabiting my new body will take some getting used to. My observing mind now has a new landscape with which to familiarize itself. I am looking forward to getting to know my new self and keeping company with my old self. As I integrate these two, I will be creating a new pathway for my own aging.

WHERE HAS PREDICTABILITY GONE?

Originally published September 1, 2019

THIS HAS BEEN A HARD week! Always looking for common threads, I gathered a few and just started to unravel them a bit. The threads are these: "I can't seem to get a grip anymore." "Things are going by so quickly." "There doesn't seem to be any firm ground underneath me anymore." And my favorite (from a patient): "Molecules of crazy are raining down." My unraveling of these has given me a chance to slow down my own mental treadmill. So I decided to look at the content of my thoughts, feelings, beliefs, and behaviors—the four cornerstones of cognitive behavioral therapy.

Habit is a useful strategy, but it can also create blind spots. Here's what I mean. I suspect you have all experienced something like the following at one time or another. You are driving to a specific location (say your drugstore). Your mind is thinking, "I'll just stop by the post office and pick up some stamps, then I'll go by cleaners since it's on the way, and then I'll treat myself to a cup of coffee . . ." and by that time the turnoff for the drugstore is in your rear-view mirror, and the car is heading to the coffee shop of its own volition. This is habit.

Habits are Unconscious

The problem with habit is that it is, by definition, unconscious! And while it can be useful not to have to focus and think about some things (such as remembering the sequence of starting your car), habit can be problematic when we miss the turnoff for our destination. The same thing happens with positive and negative thoughts.

When the content of our thoughts is negative, then the negative thoughts take over. When our feelings respond to those negative thoughts (crying or feeling blue, irritable, or angry), our behaviors reflect our thoughts (driving aggressively; saying mean things; sleeping, eating, or drinking too much). These behaviors conspire to either validate or challenge beliefs we have about ourselves ("I am/am not a nice person"; "I am/am not calm and quiet"; "I can/can't control my eating/drinking/etc."). It's truly a vicious cycle.

This system of thoughts, feelings, beliefs, and behaviors is influenced by what I listen to (TV and radio), whom I associate with (friends, family, coworkers), what people of influence and authority are telling me (parents, teachers, religious people, news media, police, elected officials), and what capacity I have to take in all this input. This last part is important.

Capacity to Manage

How much capacity I have to manage my thoughts, feelings, beliefs, and behaviors varies from day to day and sometimes from moment to moment. When I am rested, well-fed, well-exercised, and hanging out with people I love and who love me, my capacity is *huge*. When I come home after a day of work feeling tired, hungry, and unappreciated, then my capacity goes down. If you live alone, have chronic pain, or are dealing with illness and despair, then your capacity may be even less. Add financial worries, feelings of low self-esteem, and being someone on the outside, and you may find the well is dry.

My point here is that we all need to be working on building our capacities. We need more love, more tolerance, more compassion, more space, more time, more happiness. We need space to breathe and think without being told how and what. We need to forgive ourselves more quickly and forgive others just as quickly. We need to find ways to support each other instead of tear each other down.

Helping Each Other

The only way we are going to make it in this world is if we help each other. In spite of all our cultural directives to be independent, that strategy works only in the short haul.

I feel an urgency and a call to action that hasn't been present for several generations. Boomers were tasked with asking not what our country could do for us, but what we could do for our country. That invitation now extends to the world. As aging Americans, we have been blessed with peace, incredible prosperity, and the promise that we would not have to struggle. We have an obligation to extend that legacy to our children, grandchildren, and the communities we live in. If I don't find a way to manage the negative content that currently fills the airwaves, I will become frozen and unable to contribute and change my habits. My capacity to act and effect change will become less and less.

Taking Responsibility for Ourselves

I am not suggesting that each of us take on the whole world. I am suggesting that each of us pay attention to our thoughts, feelings, beliefs, and behaviors. Take responsibility for increasing your capacity to care for yourself and then care for others who are in your life. This effort may look like smiling at the grocery checkout clerk, or having a conversation with someone you don't know. Or holding a door open for someone who is moving more slowly or needs extra help. Or taking flowers to a sick friend, or baking cookies and taking them to a meeting. Or inviting two or three people to your home, listening to music, and having a cup of coffee or tea. Or picking apples from a neighbor's tree (with permission!) and sharing them with others.

Truly, small acts of kindness have powerful effects on the giver and receiver. I may not be able to put out the fires in the Amazon, but I can write my elected officials and ask that they take a stand for the good of Mother Earth. I may not be able to address economic imbalance, but I can leave a generous tip when I go to a restaurant. And if you can't do any of these things, I invite you to just appreciate who you are and the differences you have made in the lives of people you love.

Transforming into Possible

The threads I started with at the beginning seem more manageable when I look at them through this lens.

"I can't seem to get a grip anymore" can be transformed into *"I have to let go of some of my responsibilities and let others help me."*

"Things are going by so quickly" can be transformed into *"It's time to stop and smell the roses."*

"There doesn't seem to be any firm ground underneath me anymore" can be transformed into *"Change is a*

challenge. I'm not sure what's ahead, but I have made it this far."

And, last but not least, *"Molecules of crazy are raining down"* can be transformed into *"Lucy in the Sky with Diamonds."*

JUMP! FROGGY JUMP!
A CAUTIONARY TALE

Originally published September 8, 2019

BACK IN THE DAYS WHEN there were only three major networks and news was something you got by reading a newspaper or listening to the radio, how you figured out what was going on depended on whom you trusted. I grew up in Chicago in the 1950s and 1960s. My family read the *Chicago Tribune* and the *Sun Times* and we watched *The Huntley-Brinkley Report* or Walter Cronkite's *CBS Evening News* on TV. These were all we needed. We drew conclusions about what was going on based on what these trusted sources of information told us and what we saw before our very own eyes.

More and more we are expected to rely on our own judgment and draw conclusions without solid facts. Nowadays, there are thousands of sources of "information," some of which are just plain malarkey and some of which have basis in fact. There are all kinds of talking heads out there, and as a "consumer" I am expected to sort through the dross and find the golden threads of truth. And here is where the problem lies. Let's face it—human beings are notorious for drawing wrong conclusions.

I had a professor in grad school who taught us that the scientific method is all about making observations and measurements and then drawing conclusions. He used the following experiment to illustrate these principles.

This experiment was designed to see how far a frog can jump. No animals were actually harmed in this experiment.

Title: Measures of stimulus and response in determining normative distance covered by *Anura Neobatrachia* in a controlled condition.

Step 1: Weigh and measure frog. Place frog in jumping area. Say, "Jump! Froggy Jump!" and measure how far the frog jumps.

Step 2: Remove front left leg. Place frog in jumping area. Say, "Jump! Froggy Jump!" and measure how far the frog jumps.

Step 3: Remove front right leg. Place frog in jumping area. Say, "Jump! Froggy Jump!" and measure how far the frog jumps.

Step 4: Remove rear left leg. Place frog in jumping area. Say, "Jump! Froggy Jump!" and measure how far the frog jumps.

Step 5: Remove rear right leg. Place frog in jumping area. Say, "Jump! Froggy Jump!" and measure how far the frog jumps.

Here's how the experiment was written up:

Initial measurement frog jumped 330 centimeters.

Second measurement frog jumped 150 centimeters (veering left).

Third measurement frog jumped 120 centimeters (no veering).

Fourth measurement frog jumped 8 centimeters (veering left).

Fifth measurement frog jumped 0 centimeters with following notation: Instructions repeated 3Xs. No response noted from frog.

What do you imagine the conclusion of this experiment was? I won't keep you in suspense:

"Conclusion: Frogs with no legs are deaf."

And this, dear readers, is the dilemma we currently face.

Critical Thinking

I was reading a respected news source that was talking about how old most of our politicians are. Average age in Congress is fifty-eight for the House and sixty-four for the Senate. Those ages don't seem old to me! The conclusion the source drew was this:

A case can be made that this once energetic, generous, problem-solving American Republic is displaying signs of becoming an intolerant, reckless, regressive Gerontocracy. Our borders are closing, hate crimes are rising, markets are chaotic, the environment is ignored, allies are shunned, and enemies embraced. Our leaders, our electorate and our government are aging—it shows, and it's worrisome . . .

There's a reason we should care about an overabundance of elderly decision-makers at the top of our government, and it boils down to biology. On average, human cognitive functioning declines dramatically after age 70, and the types of intelligence that decline most sharply are "the capacity to absorb large amounts of new information and data in a short time span and apply it to solve problems in unaccustomed fashion." ("American Gothic: Reverse Ageism in American Politics," *Daily PNut*, September 5, 2019)

Right Data/Wrong Conclusions

I think this is a case of concluding that frogs with no legs are deaf. One of the challenges of making a statement such as "on average, human cognitive functioning declines dramatically after age 70" is that it implies that that old people are cognitively unfit. I suggest this conclusion has more to do with ageism and stereotyping than actual evidence. This judgment is like concluding that frogs with no legs are deaf.

There is no doubt that older brains do things differently and may take more time to accomplish some tasks. But that doesn't mean older brains are deficient. I can think of any number of politicians who did not have high levels of functioning before they were elected and haven't improved over the years. I can also name older pols whose capacity for comprehension and ability to synthesize huge amounts of information and *come to a reasoned conclusion* based on their experience and knowledge base remains intact.

Measurement Problems

The question comes down to this: What are we measuring? If it is speed, then you can put money on younger brains doing better. But you can also put money on higher error rates. If you are measuring accuracy, older brains will more often be "right" but will take longer to achieve the answer. Quite frankly, in terms of making decisions, I prefer the latter approach.

The problem is when Americans go to the polls, we do not have access to any information on the cognitive functioning of those who want to represent us and make decisions on our behalf. We elect folks based on sound bites, personality characteristics, and our own habitual ways of thinking, including our prejudices and preferences. Nowhere in that decision-making process will you find data that would indicate whether your elected representative actually is capable of doing the job you are asking him or her to do. When you stop and think about this fact, it is downright scary!

Lack of Guidance

Our founding fathers did not have access to the methods of evaluating competence or "fitness" for office that we do today. They identified a minimum age for running for office but little else, trusting (I believe) in the collective wisdom of those who were voting to identify an able representative.

There was no consideration of how an "older brain" worked, since folks on average didn't live that long. Notable exceptions, however, were Benjamin Franklin (84), John Adams (90), and Thomas Jefferson (83). My point here is that we will always find "notable exceptions." Sam Rayburn and Tip O'Neill both ran a very tight ship in the House of Representatives when they served as speaker of the House, and they were both pretty old. My point is that age alone is not an accurate predictor of cognitive functioning.

Fitness Evaluation

So what can we do? Since there is little likelihood that voters will have access to cognitive evaluations of those running for office, I suggest the following metric when evaluating the fitness of those you are voting for:

Don't vote for candidates just because you like the way they look and sound. Check their track record and see how consistent they are.

Remember, they are running for office for a reason. Find out what that is! What kind of jobs have they had and how long have they had them?

Once you get your answers, watch out for jumping to the wrong conclusion. You might just find that you jumped farther than a deaf frog.

ENOUGH

Originally published June 3, 2018

HOW DO YOU DETERMINE YOUR self-worth as you age? Do you already know your assets and how to manage your resources? You may be thinking I am talking about finances, but I am not. I am talking about four key beliefs that aren't typically explored when it comes to planning our futures:

> **I am enough.**
> **I have enough.**
> **There is enough.**
> **That's good enough.**

I Am Enough

Knowing you are enough at any age is important, but it is foundational to how you experience yourself as you reach 60, 70, 80, or 90. How you measure your self-worth dictates the kind of old age you experience. Your sense of self-worth affects every area of aging, including how engaged you are with life, your capacity for dealing with illness and loss, your memory, your spiritual and religious practices and beliefs, your concerns and worries about your loved ones, and your fears about dying.

I am not talking about pride or egotism here. I am talking about seeing yourself as an important contributor to your friends and family, a legacy builder for those who will come after you, and a curator of the beliefs and values of those who came before.

Being "enough" is not a static goal. It requires constant adjustment to the needs of those who depend on you. It requires recalibrating based on changes in the world you live in. Knowing you are enough requires insight and reflection on the consequences of decisions made sometimes in haste or without sufficient information.

I Have Enough

What does it mean to have enough? Fundamentally it means that you have access to sufficient resources to keep you alive, housed, engaged, and participating in your community. When you are dying, having enough means having sufficient resources to adequately house you, manage your pain, and pay for medicine and hospitalization (if and when it is needed). Where those resources are located is not limited by geography, time, or ability. They are anchored in your awareness and willingness to take stock of yourself and your surroundings.

Having enough is a measure of security and belief. If you have always had access to resources, "enough" for you will be different from someone who has had to manage with less. For example, if you have always had access to food, clothing, and shelter, and your community is then devastated by a flood, you may find that your definition of "enough" changes as you reclaim your life afterward.

There Is Enough

Believing there is enough sounds quite simple, yet I cannot tell you how frequently patients share their fears with me that they will end up on the streets or will run out of money before they die. What if there isn't enough to go around? This concept is based on notions of abundance and scarcity. What you believe about these concepts is based in how you were raised and your experiences with money, choices, and ability to exercise your will.

For many of us, intense and negative feelings are associated with having or not having money. Shame, a belief that money is evil, fears associated with poverty, and life experiences in which you either gained or lost status through having a certain level of income or things—all combine to heighten your hopes and fears about aging.

I know at some point I will need the help of strangers and friends to keep me functioning. I will need to be more careful with my money because I don't know how long I will actually live. I will need to take action to ensure that the things I need such as Social Security and Medicare will be available to me and others.

I know these things because of the events I have seen unfold with family members and friends, and because I have listened as many of my patients have told me they wished they had planned better. Not all of us are planners. Most of us, though, prefer not to be surprised! What you need is a map with a tour guide showing you how you can benefit from what others just like you have learned. That way, if something similar comes up, you won't be as surprised.

Self-Worth

It has been my privilege to work with aging adults for most of my life. I have gained insight into the challenges that aging brings because my family members, patients, and friends have shared their journeys with me. What they taught me was—regardless of my background, education, religious or spiritual belief—unless I value myself first, others will not value me in the ways I need to be valued. And their valuing me has important implications as I get older.

In the face of losses—of loved ones, hearing, sight, mobility, and memory—I have learned that it is essential that I believe there is enough available to me. This belief centers on knowing there is enough love, enough care, and enough support to carry me to my end.

Loss is part of aging. Coming to terms with loss can be challenging. Given these truths, how do you hold on to the belief that there is enough? Do you think there will be enough for you as you age? How do you manage your concerns if you are sure there won't be? How do you manage your hopes, if you think there will be?

Letting Go of Things

For most of us, getting older is a process of letting go of people and things. We may downsize our living situation, attend more funerals, and find ourselves changing our beliefs and expectations about what we are capable of doing. In letting go, we are creating space for other things.

Letting go often feels frightening. Yet, until we release, there usually isn't enough room for what is wanting to replace the void. So, instead, some of us accumulate and squirrel things away in hopes that we will have what we need in the future.

Letting Go of Resentments

We make plans for all kinds of contingencies and hope our plans will be enough. While this strategy is generally a sound one, if you end up buying four or five of the same item but have no place to store these things, you will end up with not enough space. And the same holds true when you hold on to resentment, hurts, and negative feelings. There is little room left over for joy, happiness, and hope.

My wonderful mentors have shown me that believing I have enough is key to the quality of aging that can be mine. Having enough friends, laughter, quiet time—having enough faith that things will turn out not as I will them, but as I adapt to and accommodate them—remains the best formula for growing old well.

They have given me a rough map to follow, and while I will need to explore territory on my own and perhaps even blaze a few new paths, I am reassured that I have been prepared well and can adjust to what may lie ahead.

These are the assets that I believe you should preserve and invest in.

SUFFICIENT AMOUNT
FOR PURPOSE
NEEDED

Originally published January 5, 2020

THIS HOLIDAY SEASON SEEMED PARTICU-
LARLY odd to me. I had more time to myself than I
have had in several years. I had less pain than I have
had in a long time. I had more to eat and enjoyed
every morsel. I had more memories, both happy and
sad, and I had more occasions to create new memories.

I reflected on all the blessings that have come my
way in the past few years, including making new
friends, traveling more than I have done in a while,
attending more concerts, and improving my writing. I spent my time taking stock of who I am and
who I used to be, as well as thinking about how I

want to spend my time, use my skills, and explore who I am becoming.

What is Enough?

All of this is to say that what I have been contemplating is this question: What is enough? This is a very big question, and it continues to challenge me—especially since I am facing my older years without a partner and needing to rely on my skills, talents, and gifts to make sure I maintain a comfortable standard of living.

It is not easy for me to write these words, as I realize just how incredibly privileged I am to enjoy the standard of living I have. I do not take lightly the fact that it could very easily change, no matter what my intentions may be, nor am I ignorant of the fact that there are many, too many others who are daily faced with homelessness, loneliness, hunger, and fear.

The Shame of Not Having Enough

My mother experienced a great deal of anxiety and shame in her later years because she did not have enough money to support herself. The irony was that she was surrounded by antiques and lived in a house that was paid for.

She ultimately ended up qualifying for Medicaid because she had never saved her money and instead relied on mortgaging her home in an effort to cover expenses. She kept this information from me for a long time, and by the time I did find out what her situation was, she was at the point of losing her home.

Fortunately, I was able to help her out, but the result was a deep rift in our relationship and an added financial burden for me when I was just starting out in my career. I share this story not for sympathy, but to point out that a very high price was paid for not having enough.

Hierarchy of Needs

Was there a better way to have managed the situation? What do I need to do to make sure that I have enough? Abraham Maslow identified a key component in answering this question. He called it a "hierarchy of needs."

At its base he identified essential physiological needs, such as food, clothing, and shelter. Meeting these needs is critical in order for human beings to survive and attend to other needs. My mother became emotionally and psychologically frozen when she was unable to pay for her food, pay the bank, and keep the heat and lights on. She didn't have sufficient amounts for the purpose needed. She didn't have enough.

She had also lost her sense of self. Some of this loss happened as her role and status in life changed. When she was younger and was working, her world was filled with purpose and meaning. After she retired, she sought connection and community through volunteering and participating in church activities. But as her health declined, so did these activities. She wasn't able to go out as much, and she became more and more of a recluse. She no longer felt she was enough.

Changing Capacities

One of the inevitable consequences of growing old is the realization that time is running out. Other things seem to decline also. Strength and endurance change. What used to take seconds or minutes may now take hours or days. Capacity to bounce back from challenges can also change. Resilience and ability to manage stress, illness, and environmental conditions, as well as increased emotional and cognitive demands, can all vary as the decades go by. Losses of loved ones (including pets), partners, friends, classmates, and colleagues become more frequent, bringing home the reality that our time on this planet is finite. All of these factors influence our belief about whether there is enough.

A core measure of satisfaction with life—what you believe is good enough—is challenged as multiple factors change. Things that I was impatient with when I was younger, I now find easier to tolerate. Other things are no longer tolerable at all, and I become indignant when others do not share my point of view. There is an urgency to some things because I know how fragile or special they are. But how do I communicate that urgency with others who do not have the same worldview?

Working Definition of "Enough"

My working definition for "enough" is having a sufficient amount for the purpose needed. This requires me to really understand what purpose is. Do I need money to buy food, pay the mortgage or rent, or set aside for my care or the care of someone else? Do I need energy to fight illness, sustain the effort needed to take care of my activities of daily living, and focus my mind and soul on creating things? Do I need faith to confront my fears of dying, courage to defend the values and truths I hold dear, and compassion and tolerance to cool my anger and tame my desire for vengeance? What are sufficient amounts of these things?

We are at the beginning of a new decade. We shouldn't pass up this opportunity to explore what having enough means.

I challenge you to explore what it means for you to be able to say,

"I am enough."
"I have enough."
"There is enough."
"That's good enough!"

SUMMER MUSINGS

Originally published July 7, 2019

THERE ARE SO MANY THINGS that are of interest to me and need my attention—but, honestly, I'd rather be swinging in a hammock and sipping iced tea than focusing on them. This is what summer does to me. I feel entitled to move more slowly, ease into my day, and linger with the twilight before giving up and going to bed.

This experience is paired with the astonishing awareness that time is passing, oh, so quickly. My week starts on a Monday and, within seconds, it seems it is already Friday. Weekends look clear on my calendar but are filled with events (including naps!) and errands that never seem to get done during the week.

To-Do Lists

With the best of intentions, I make to-do lists that I eventually find buried under other papers and end up recycling, since few got ta-done. I am easily distracted going through boxes of old papers and photographs, only to find my back aching from sitting too long and my memory banks overflowing with recalling events from long ago. Newer memories are still being made, but not at the rate the old ones seem to have accumulated.

I had house guests recently who allowed me the joy of showing off where I live. Northern California has destination points, fine dining, exquisite photo opportunities, and lots and lots of music and art. The area is anchored by San Francisco Bay, not to mention that jewel of a city. In taking folks for a drive through these areas, I got to relive forty years of memories.

When Past is Present

I laughed (mostly to myself, but occasionally out loud) as I drove through neighborhoods where I had lived, noting changes in storefronts and architecture while filtering it all through the lens of past adventures. There were still places that remained relatively unchanged, and other areas that seemed totally foreign to me.

Sharing all this with friends who had never before seen San Francisco or the Sonoma coast was a delightful experience. I realized how much information I had accumulated. I realized how much I like to talk about people, places, and events associated with different locations. I realized just how much I love where I live.

Where Will I Live?

Because my guests were of similar age, we discussed the changes we will need to make in the next few years. Inevitably, the question of where to live came up. Geography isn't the only criterion for deciding where to live as I age. But geography plays a huge role. Try as I might, it is incredibly difficult for me to find comparable geography to where I live now.

Since children and grandchildren are not in my picture, I don't feel any pull to move closer to them. But I understand why those who do have extended family would want to be close. This variable is a double-edged sword, however. The older we get, the less able we are to move. It is far more likely that your children and grandchildren will be moving, potentially leaving you in a community where you haven't had time to grow roots. For some, this eventuality may not be problematic, but for others, it may result in isolation.

There are three losses that we have to face as we age: loss of place, loss of person, and loss of purpose. I have already dealt with loss of persons dear to me. I am fortunate to have a strong sense of purpose that I hope and trust will carry me through my elderhood. But the sticking point for me is loss of place.

Moving Day

Having lived in my home for twenty-two-plus years, and having lived in California for forty, I cannot imagine leaving this state. I have taken trips to Washington State, Montana, Arizona, and New Mexico to see how they "feel." And while each state has its benefits, it also has drawbacks. Finding that sweet spot is challenging.

I figure I have one or two more years in which I could move my business and myself to a new location. In making this move, I would need to exert far more energy to make new friends, establish contacts, and set up a support network than I have done in years. This prospect actually weighs more heavily on me than the economics. It is not that I couldn't find a cheaper place to live—it's that I would pay a higher price for saving a few bucks.

Running Out

The danger most of us Boomers face, and the fear so many express to me, is outliving our savings. If what I read in financial guides is true, none of us has saved enough. That fact raises the ugly specter of becoming a bag lady or having to move in with others (possibly even family). For those who have been prudent, this prospect may be less enervating, but it is still a factor affecting our quality of life.

You can find all kinds of calculators online to help you determine how much money you will need as you age. I wish there were something similar to support all of us in determining the quality of life we want as we age.

It is important that we look at finding purpose and meaning to carry us through the years after we have "retired." It is essential that we develop skills that will help us adapt to the changes aging brings. We need to maintain levels of engagement physically, cognitively, socially, and spiritually. Inevitably, we will face our mortality. For some of us, that will bring awareness to the spiritual aspects of our lives. Each of these is a pillar that will support us as we age.

TOO LITTLE;
TOO LATE

Originally published January 19, 2020

THE START OF A NEW YEAR brings with it my re-
commitment to achieving financial stability. I am
like one of those people who sign up for gym mem-
berships in January and by February have given up
on going but haven't stopped the automatic pay-
ments from my checking account. The year 2020 has
been no exception. I have committed to learning as
much as I can about retirement since it is now on
the near horizon for me. But I am finding it might
be too little, too late.

There are plenty of sources to choose from that
warn me of the dire outcomes if I fail to put sufficient money aside. There is no end of blogs,
podcasts, and online and TV ads for companies that

will ensure a good return on my extra income as I age. They invite me to put my hard-earned money into their trusted hands and then just go off and exercise at the gym or take a cruise or indulge in a newfound hobby.

Money and Emotion

Money is one of those things that carries with it a *huge* emotional charge for me, yet I know money is only a number. How I feel about my money seems to have less to do with the actual amount than the narrative I recite to myself.

Depending on that story, I can feel ashamed that I do not have enough or guilty that I have so much. I can tell myself I "should" be doing more investing or that I need to watch my pennies. I have long, involved dialogues about how and why I haven't saved for my retirement. I have soliloquies that rival Shakespeare about how I was underpaid and underappreciated, and why I am worthy of winning the Publisher's Clearinghouse or the lottery but won't play because it is rigged. I am awaiting a Pulitzer for my work!

The numbers themselves are merely metrics. If I have enough coming in to cover my rent, my utilities, my groceries, and my mortgage, then I am doing well. If I don't, then I am in trouble. Knowing how much is coming and in going out seems to be the key to this whole thing. The goal is to have more coming in than going out. See—I am a financial wizard!

Sources of Money

What has changed dramatically for those born just before World War II (which includes many of us now approaching or in early retirement) is the source of our money. Social Security was signed into law in 1935. This was in response to the cataclysmic effects of the Great Depression, causes of which included a wealth distribution gap, an unregulated banking industry and stock market, environmental catastrophes, and lack of government oversight and enforcement. (Sound familiar?)

Employment trends shifted dramatically in this country in the last half of the twentieth century and, along with that shift, who contributes to the retirement pot changed. Prior to World War II, most Americans worked for themselves on farms or in small businesses. After World War II, more Americans became employed by corporations like General Motors or Ma Bell.

Workers produced different goods in different amounts and enjoyed higher salaries and job security in white-collar jobs. The companies paid a fair wage as a result of the hard work of labor unions and promised a retirement benefit. In exchange for showing up on time and working hard for twenty-five or thirty years for the same company, workers came to expect their employer would pay them even after they stopped working.

The Legacy of the New Deal

Americans over the age of sixty-five were also guaranteed a specific return on their "investment" (Federal Insurance Contributions Act, or FICA, taxes paid toward Social Security and Medicare) over and above anything their employers might offer.

This was a sweet deal during the boom years of full employment and huge corporate profits. That this money was essentially put in an investment account for each employee seems to have benefited a lot of Americans over the years. And before someone got the notion that individuals could do better investing for themselves.

A Change in Perception

After Americans elected Ronald Reagan, things changed. Social Security began to be called an entitlement program rather than a savings program. As the strength and influence of unions declined, companies dramatically changed their retirement and benefits offerings. After the recession in the 1980s, many employees were left without guaranteed retirement benefits at all and were encouraged to start investing themselves in things called annuities, individual retirement accounts (IRAs), and 401(k)s.

Throughout the 1980s and 1990s, distribution of wealth continued to drift away from the middle class. The result is the popular culture defining the 98 percent as besieged and holding the 2 percent responsible for most of our economic woes.

Over these decades, however, financial behavior hasn't changed much. For those who have excess income, the primary financial behavior is to invest. For those who live paycheck to paycheck, the primary financial behavior is to rely on Social Security or keep on working, depending on family, government services, and support or charity to make up whatever gap exists. Because there is the population bubble, however, a greater number of boomers may find themselves needing to rely on different sources of income once they stop working.

A Harsh Reality

According to the "401k Specialist," 42 percent of boomers "have absolutely nothing saved." The implications of this fact are not complex. As a matter of fact, they are as clear as that "E" on the eye chart. There are approximately seventy-four million boomers in the United States today. That means thirty-one million not only will be drawing down their Social Security but also will need to tap into local, state and federal services, as well as charities, for support after these boomers stop working.

Where are the funds going to come from to keep those among us who own property from foreclosure? Where is the expanded public housing being built to house those of us who can no longer live independently? Where are the medical providers who will need to accept Medicare or Medicaid insurance?

Who will feed us? Why aren't our duly elected officials putting these issues front and center?

Too Little; Too Late

Even though I have some money set aside, I count myself among those in that 42 percent. My plan to address my financial vulnerabilities includes working until I can't, putting as much money aside as I can, and trusting that government services will be available to me. Based on what I am seeing, reading, and feeling, this plan is too little and too late.

While most financial planning is directed at younger investors, the basics remain the same. Here is a link to a great article in Lifehacker with nested links that might give you a leg up!

SOUNDS ABOUND

Originally published July 14, 2019

I JUST GOT NEW HEARING aids, and they are amazing! I got my first set after a long period of denial. In my late thirties I noticed my left ear was filled with that buzzing and whistling sound called tinnitus (pronounced "tin-uh-tis"). I sort of got used to it and was able to ignore it most of the time. Then my right ear started to get the same noises, and I noticed I was having difficulty understanding people in crowds. I went along with this problem for more than ten years.

I attributed all my tinnitus to listening to too much rock and roll on the handy transistor radio that I hid under my pillow at night when I was a teenager. I just kept going along and not really noticing that I was missing out on much—but I really was.

Surprise! You Have A Brain Tumor!

What finally got me to the hearing specialist was a bout of vertigo. The dizziness was attributed to the crystals in my inner ear, which had gotten out of whack. The doctor had me in a special chair that reclined. He partly inverted me and turned my head back and forth, in a movement kind of like one of those lava lamp wave machines (mute your sound), until the spinning subsided.

I didn't really think much of all this until he recommended that I also have an MRI (magnetic resonance imaging). Some people get anxiety with this kind of procedure. I am lucky. I don't. As a matter of fact, I find this whole thing very interesting!

So I went for the MRI and waited for the results. It was confirmed that I had a brain! What was also confirmed was that I had a tumor on my left acoustic nerve. This is known as an acoustic neuroma and is relatively rare. Having found this, the recommendation was that I have it removed. In other words, I needed to have brain surgery.

Thank You, but No Thank You!

Seeing as I am a seasoned professional, and one who deals with all kinds of brain disorders, I did what most of you would have done (I am guessing here). I Googled "acoustic neuroma," read all the scary testimonials, and went into denial for more than a year. I was *not* going to have brain surgery!

The reason I was so sure was that my insurance at the time was with a large, managed care provider that organized care within its network. Neurology surgery was done in a hospital more than sixty miles away. The procedure would have required that I go to the facility, be admitted, and have my head opened up, the neuroma "stripped" from the nerve, and a drain inserted into my brain, followed by a recovery period of approximately six weeks.

I wasn't thrilled with the idea of having to leave town to have the surgery done, much less the six-week recovery period. Oh, and I wasn't thrilled with the idea of having a brain drain, either. So I did nothing for a year.

Putting Things Off

Now I don't recommend waiting a year for surgery, especially it if is something that can restore you to full functioning. But I know it is not at all unusual for people to go into denial and avoid the prospect that surgery often brings up: mortality, possibility of poor outcome, fear of all kinds of things. Here is where I put in a plug for talking with a therapist or counselor. S/he can help you deal with the anxiety or denial and assist you in making the right decision for you.

Instead, I utilized several alternative methods for coping with this slow-growing, benign tumor. I tried visualizations (shrinking that tumor, zapping it with imaginary laser beams, dissolving it with white light). I changed my diet. I kept reading about neuromas. And, finally, I changed my health insurance.

Location, Location, Location

This last step got me to the threshold of a most remarkable experience. I am very lucky to live in an area of the country that has top-notch research institutions. In this case, I got a referral to the

University of California, San Francisco (UCSF) neurology clinic. There, the doctors validated the findings of the original MRI, now a year old, took some new shots, and determined I was a candidate for gamma-ray knife surgery.

This would entail my coming into the hospital early in the morning, being fitted with a titanium "crown" that would be locked into a machine that looks like an open MRI, and then be strategically blasted with short bursts of gamma rays. I would be able to leave the same day and not have to worry about a brain drain, because no incision would be made.

I am blessed with friends who knew a lot about UCSF because of their own remarkable story (a successful heart transplant). These friends took me early one morning for my procedure. I looked stunning with my titanium crown and sat around for hours while the surgical team mapped out my surgery. Finally, I was loaded into the machine, my crown affixed to the table, and I meditated for the next thirty minutes. No sounds, no feeling of heat or pain, no muss, no fuss, just a great thirty-minute meditation. Once done, I was released from my crown, assisted in sitting up, joined by the neurology team, and sent home.

Post-Op

The surgery was successful; however, the damage to my acoustic nerve was such that only a little of its functioning was able to be preserved. It is not clear whether more could have been preserved if I hadn't waited that year.

This damage is what led me to getting hearing aids. My first set made me realize just how much I had been missing. I was able to understand conversations without having to stare at the person's face and strain to understand them. I no longer nodded sagely when someone said something I couldn't understand, and the instances I totally missed what was said and embarrassed myself with a wrong guess dropped precipitously.

I would go in for my annual hearing test and was pleased with how the hearing aids helped me to adapt to my hearing loss. The only drawback was that the hearing aids were incredibly expensive.

Hearing Aids Are Essential

This issue continues to be a barrier for so many people in getting hearing aids. Most private insurance plans cover only a small percentage of the actual cost. Medicare covers nothing. While this lack of coverage makes no sense for an aging population, it continues to be the sad reality.

In the years since I got my first set of hearing aids, the technology has improved by leaps and bounds. I now have a choice of programs that can cancel background noise, accommodate different kinds of locations (such as noisy restaurants, movie theater, one-on-one conversations), and are now paired with my smartphone. All these improvements go a long way in keeping me literally "in the game."

Studies support what is common sense—if you can hear more, you can engage more. People who stay engaged have better cognitive functioning and overall are happier.

I encourage all of you to at least get a hearing test. Yes, you will be offered the opportunity to purchase hearing aids if your hearing is found to be diminishing. Get the information and don't worry about the sales pitch. Do get the hearing aids when you can, if needed. You are worth the investment. It will pay big dividends as you age.

TEACHING OLD DOGS NEW TECHNOLOGIES

Originally published July 28, 2019

Technology proved to be a lifesaver for many of us during the pandemic. I very rarely hear people saying, "I can't do that!" anymore. I do hear a preference for in-person contact, but having just gotten off a Zoom call this morning with a group of writers who are all over seventy, this notion that old dogs can't learn new tricks just doesn't hold up!

I RECENTLY PURCHASED A BRAND-new Nikon D3500 camera. I have great aspirations of becoming a video producer of quality educational products and decided I needed to come into the twenty-first century. My new camera looks suspiciously like my old Canon 35mm from back in the day. But it is anything but!

The manual for my Nikon D3500 is 345 pages long. There are obviously very important facts and findings concealed within, but pulling out the goodies is daunting! So I turned to YouTube.

Learning Styles

Now, being the age I am, I was taught to learn new skills by reading and following step-by-step instructions. Some of you may be familiar with the concept of learning styles. In brief, some of us learn by watching and doing, some by reading and doing, and some by just doing the thing over and over until we figure it out. I fall into the latter category and have reluctantly adapted my style to at least reading about what is supposed to be done. But mostly I try things out.

Should you be like me, may I just encourage you to forget about using the exploration method with these newfangled cameras—I have needed to read, watch YouTube, try stuff out, and then go back and do all three over and over again. I am not sure whether this is just my brain not being able to grasp all the bells and whistles or being unable to learn from watching fifteen-year-old geniuses explain how to operate the camera. Maybe it is a combination of both.

Newer Is Not Always Easier

I admit to being impatient. I want to be making movies, but there are some basics I need to learn before I can start doing that. Back in the old days, I used to point, click, and shoot. Now, I have to load batteries, slip in memory chips, go through fifteen menus to choose the right settings, and then turn the damn thing on. So far, I have had to return the wrong battery, the wrong memory chip, and the wrong microphone. Amazon returns and I are getting to be great buds!

While technology is challenging, I am intrigued with how much difference it can make in the lives of aging adults. Several years ago, I became aware of the availability of smart technology to make older adults who live with memory loss safer.

One of the challenges with some folks with dementia is that they wander. One company came up with the idea of putting GPS chips in shoes so that wanderers could be tracked. When first developed, these advances were insanely expensive, making them out of reach for most people. Today, the GPS chips and monitoring devices have come down substantially in price.

A Telling Tale

I can attest to the wonders that technology brings to aging adults. One of my patients has experienced the frightening consequence of not remembering to take his medications as directed. Like many others, he had his pills set up on a weekly basis. His habit was to sit down on Friday night, line up all the pills that needed to be taken the following week, and fill up the pill case. Also, like so many others, he had his pills mailed to him in three-month quantities (much cheaper for the pharmaceutical company).

Only problem was his primary care provider and other specialists had changed his medications over time and he couldn't remember what he needed to take for what when.

What's Wrong with This Picture?

By the time I started working with him, he had been sent to a memory specialist who had seen him on a day when he had taken his meds incorrectly and who ended up diagnosing him with a severe memory problem. My patient was ashamed, scared, and feeling quite defeated.

I had a feeling, though, that he really didn't have a memory problem. So I took a look at his meds and asked him how he managed them. His answer made me think that what might be at the bottom of his behaviors was related more to his medications and their effects than his cognitive functioning.

Technology to the Rescue

So we got him a Siri. He was used to using his iPhone. The only challenge with Siri was getting his Wi-Fi provider to hook things up correctly. Once that was settled and he had gotten used to talking to a machine, we set up reminders for him to take his medications, along with reminders about which medications he was supposed to be taking.

Within two weeks, his cognitive functioning had improved, and he was well on the way to feeling better about himself. What remains a barrier, however, is how to make the learning curve less challenging.

High-Tech; High-Touch

In one of my previous professional lives, I worked at SRI International. This is a think tank in Menlo Park, California, that has given us many different kinds of technology that today are considered commonplace. One of the conferences SRI sponsored back in the 1990s was entitled "High-Tech; High-Touch." The theme was to explore the needs that technology could address while taking into consideration human aspects. I've never forgotten this theme.

There are so many issues that aging adults will need to adapt to and find accommodations for in the twenty-first century. These are at last becoming a focus of research in gerontology. According to editors at SAGE Journals:

> For the aging population, technology is a double-edged sword. On the one hand, the rapid pace of development and change can make it difficult for older adults to learn new technologies, while the world's increasing use of and dependence on smart devices and digital technologies leaves those who struggle to

adapt at a distinct, isolated disadvantage. On the other hand, technologies geared specifically towards an increasing, aging population contribute to increased comfort and dignity, the ability to live at home for longer, ease with managing health issues, and even longer life. (Hannah R. Marston and Charles Musselwhite, "Special Collection on Aging and Technology," Gerontology and Geriatric Medicine)

We can do so much more with technology. As noted at that conference at SRI so many decades ago, we need to pair the technology with hands-on care and help. It is this intersection that fascinates me as well as currently challenging me.

What I have learned is that I need to take more time before I catch on to some new technology. Attitude is everything. Being willing to try something new makes a difference in how many of my memory neurons fire sufficiently to remember what sequence and pattern I need to follow to get the outcome I desire. Giving myself permission to relax and ask for help has made a world of difference.

MOURNING IN AMERICA

Originally published November 17, 2019

I ATTENDED A WONDERFUL MEMORIAL service this past weekend. It coincided with the Veterans Day holiday, so there was a tie-in to that national acknowledgment of loss and sacrifice. It got me to thinking about the rituals of death and how these are changing.

My first experience of death was on Thanksgiving in 1956, when my paternal grandfather had a heart attack in our home. According to stories, I asked whether Grandpa had gone to heaven, but truly, I don't remember much else of what must have been a very trying event. Of course, there must have been a funeral, but I was too young to attend such a solemn affair.

My next experience was a few years later, when I was ten. My maternal grandmother died, also of a heart attack. This funeral was held in her hometown at a funeral home run by friends of the family. It was an open casket, but I was not allowed to look in.

Five Funerals and a Viewing

I have two memories from this experience. First, as a curious but wary observer, I remember watching the adults from a small alcove away from the viewing area and seeing my grandfather crying unashamedly. The second memory, oddly, was of being given chocolate nonpareils as a way of keeping me quiet and happy.

After the viewing, we joined the motorcade out to the grave site and said our goodbyes as the casket was lowered into the ground on the family plot. This was followed by a huge gathering at our family home where all sorts of people came to share stories about my grandmother.

In the years that followed, we continued the custom of visiting the cemetery on holidays to lay flowers on her grave, tidy up the other family tombstones as well, and generally commune with family members who had gone before.

Death of My Father

Within a few more years, my father died. His funeral was much different and far more emotionally imprinted on my memory. Not so much for the actual service, but for the embarrassment I felt in the receiving line when my grandmother, out of her own grief wailed in front of everybody, "My boy! My boy!"

I was fourteen at the time and had shut down emotionally around my father's illness and death. As a teenager, my grandmother's acting out in public was incredibly socially embarrassing to me and stays with me to this day. That day it more than overcame any grief I felt at my father's dying. My father was cremated. His ashes were put in a mausoleum. Curiously, I have never been to visit his resting place.

More Death

I was with my maternal grandfather when he received last rites, although he didn't actually pass for several weeks. The same family undertakers who did the work on my grandmother took care of his remains. This time I made sure I looked in the casket. It was a handsome casket; expensive wood, quilted and tufted interior with silk pleats. Truly a worthy resting place for a man of my grandfather's standing.

His service was conducted at the Catholic church where he had been an altar boy; from there the funeral cortege made its way down Main Street. The family story is that halfway through town, a Schlitz beer delivery truck joined the funeral procession. We all thought this appropriate since my grandfather definitely enjoyed his glass of beer!

Clusters of Dying

For many years after these deaths, I was spared more family funerals. Then, like a cluster of storms, my mother died, my husband died, and my cousin died. My mother had decided to "give her body to science"; however, after her death at age eighty-nine, emaciated, and in the later stages of dementia, science said, "No, thank you." So I was left to figure out what to do. I somehow did not have the time, money, or energy to commit her body to the ground in the style of her parents.

The same family who had buried my grandparents were no longer in business, so I engaged another funeral home.

I was shown around the viewing room filled with caskets, offered examples of the latest in jewelry that could be made to contain the ashes of my loved one, and informed of the costs involved in laying my mother to rest. I can still remember the conflicted feelings of wanting to give my mother a grand send-off but having to accept the fact that I did not have the financial resources to do so.

I also did not have time to put together a memorial service, which to this day has left me feeling quite guilty. Instead, my mother's ashes sat on a shelf in the mortuary until I was able to return and get her a headstone. She was finally interred on a hot and humid summer's day while I and a cousin, the only two witnesses to her last good-bye, were eaten alive by mosquitoes.

One More Good-Bye

My husband was clear that he wanted to be cremated and have his ashes spread in the ocean. This we accomplished with his children and grandchildren at a favorite beach on a lovely August afternoon.

I kept some of his ashes aside, as I had promised him that I would also take him "home" to his favorite place in the Adirondacks, on Lake George where he had spent many happy summers as a child. In making this pilgrimage, I stopped off at his parents' grave in Westport, Connecticut, to pay my respects.

Some twenty years earlier, my husband and I had visited that gravesite and cut back an evergreen shrub that had taken root and obscured their headstones. It remained visible and free of growth, although I have no idea who was tending to it.

What I Have Learned

What I have learned from all these experiences is that it is important to recognize and ritualize what happens after someone dies. Having a memorial service allows people to gather and remember but also to close the circle of that relationship.

The staid script of a funeral mass or a graveside blessing marks the departure line between those of us tasked with continuing to live and those who no longer share this life with us. It is a place, geographic and emotional, that can be revisited as needed.

Shared grief is an important step in the mourning process. Receiving the kind words and offers of sympathy may be taxing for the widow or widower, but it is also a balm for the living.

I don't know how my remains will be handled. I have no children to mourn my passing or make decisions on where to distribute my ashes. Thanks to the foresight of my ancestors, I have a spot in the family plot that is there if I need to use it. I suspect I will put some money aside and see about having my ashes planted with a tree. (Google *capsula mundi* for more information on this form of burial.)

LET'S ALL JUST TAKE A BREATH

Originally published March 29, 2020

I FREQUENTLY USE THE WORD "normal" to mean familiar and unquestioned. Just a couple of weeks ago, everything seemed predictable. All that certainly changed while I was gone on my vacation. Nothing seems familiar or unquestioned right now. Nothing seems "normal."

It would be a logical fallacy to equate my leaving the country with the increase in chaos as reported in the media, although it appears that there are some who would make that causal connection. I find taking a breath has become my primary strategy in managing my environment. Taking a breath is a very effective technique to address the floating anxiety. Taking a breath has given me back some control.

Finding the Space In Between

Pausing is an equally essential skill. Before COVID-19 took over our world, my experience of time was like watching a train passing at full speed. For those of you who have never seen a train, the cars are separate, but at high speeds they appear to blend into one solid object. You cannot see the space between cars when they are moving at high speed.

While I had become used to the incessant merging of one activity into another that has been life in the twenty-first century thus far, it was taking a toll on me that I don't think I fully appreciated until I left for my trip.

Once I was away from the demands of a private practice, managing a small business, and trying to stay on top of laundry, grocery shopping and doing my taxes, the spaces between the cars started to reappear. I began to notice my breathing. I began to notice the space between my in breath and out breath.

For those of you not familiar with meditation, these are some of the first skills taught when learning to meditate: Noticing the breath. Noticing what it feels like to inhale. Noticing what it feels like to exhale. Slowing down and putting both intention and attention around them. The trick here is not to become better at breathing in and out; rather it is to become better at noticing.

Pay Attention!

The consequences of paying attention are many. Just think about all the things you have noticed since COVID-19 has forced you to pay attention! How frequently you wash your hands; the essential need for toilet paper; just how far six feet actually is; how much stuff you have in your closets! Routines that once were unquestioned are now opportunities for exploring alternative strategies for getting needs met. Our brains are getting a workout and so are our hearts.

I was out of the United States for fifteen days. In that short period of time, an unseen virus shut down countries, caused businesses worldwide to revamp their game plans, forced governments to come together and face a new reality, and slowed life down to a crawl. When I returned from Australia, the airport was a ghost town. Few cars were on the roads. People were out walking. These were sights I hadn't experienced since I was growing up in the late 1950s and early 1960s!

Underlying Tensions

The underlying tensions of "faster," "better," "more," escalating, palpitating, demanding, louder, "me! me! me!" had dissipated, and what was left was spaciousness. I acknowledge that for some people, this spaciousness can actually feel threatening. For me, it was a welcome relief!

Interestingly, this spaciousness is similar to what I experience when I meditate. My thoughts slow down. My mind relaxes, and my inner peripheral vision opens up. I begin to experience things other than the frenetic synaptic leap from one thought to another. My need to "do" decreases as my enjoyment of "being" increases. My breathing slows down.

I have to believe that this is a good thing.

On Home Quarantine

I have not noticed a great deal of difference from how I lived my life before I left since coming home and being on self-quarantine, with one marked exception. The tension is gone. I don't mean that I am not concerned about COVID-19; of course I am. But I have seen with my own eyes how people can quickly change habits and take steps to lower risk of exposure.

I realize that many people are scared since their jobs and livelihoods are no longer guaranteed. I am hopeful, though, that these fears will be decreased as we find ways of connecting and supporting one another. We will be forced to change how we do things, and we will be making mistakes along the way.

Still, there are many wise people among us who have experienced challenges and understand that sometimes it is better to just pause briefly, catch our breath, reset, and then move forward. And there seems to be no end to the creativity that folks are tapping into as they navigate these new and challenging waters!

Optimist, Yes! Pollyanna, No!

I am, by nature and preference, an optimist. I am not, however, a Pollyanna. We are going to be asked to make changes to how we think, do things, and relate to one another. These will not be easy to do or sustain. Many of us have to relearn patience; for some, it will be a totally new experience to defer gratification for more than a few moments. Yet these are the skills that we must bring to bear if we are to be successful in a post-COVID-19 world.

It is a sad truth that many will die in this pandemic. The virus has little respect for how much money you make, where you went to school, whom you know, or what God you pray to. The virus is single-minded and purposeful—find a host and replicate. From what is known now about this process, fierce adherence to washing hands (top and bottom) with soap, using hand sanitizer, doing self-quarantine, and keeping personal distance seem to be effective in slowing the virus in its search for hosts.

It is also a sad truth that too many people, out of ignorance or lack of options, will take actions that actually increase their exposure to the virus. These actions may in turn put more of us at risk.

It is hard not to judge or condemn these people, but that will do nothing to make the world safer or free from COVID-19. I encourage you to decline the invitation to blame. Save that energy for more creative actions.

Silver Linings?

Several people have commented that the silver lining of this pandemic is that Earth is getting a time out. There are reports that the canals in Venice are clear and dolphins have returned to swim in them. Pollution monitoring in China has shown dramatic drops in particulate matter in the air over Hubei Province. While toilet paper and spaghetti may temporarily be in short supply, there is ample evidence that these staples will be replenished if we can just be patient.

In the meantime, please wash your hands and just take a breath!

RELAPSE AND RECOVERY

Originally published May 3, 2020

THERE ARE DISTINCT TENSIONS BEING felt and expressed in multiple ways right now. There is the tension of COVID-19 with all its unknowns. There is the tension rising from being told what to do by authority and not wanting to do it. There is the tension of economic uncertainty. And there is the tension of not knowing when this pandemic will be over.

To any of us who have tried to acquire a new habit, these tensions are all too familiar. I remember when I was trying to quit smoking. I knew it was bad for me and that I needed to stop. I understood at a theoretical level that stopping would involve changing lots of things. I knew it was going to be challenging. And it took me multiple attempts to achieve my goal.

At the Beginning

I had to go through stages in order to actually achieve the end result. I first had to admit that there was a problem. Once I did, I had to think about whether I actually, truly, really, really, really wanted to quit (I didn't!). Then I had to prepare to give up smoking. Preparation entailed getting rid of all the paraphernalia that went along with the habit, including the lighters, the ashtrays, and the matchbook collections. I also had to set a date to quit.

Then I finally did. I stopped! But, oh, how I wanted to go back to smoking. I would fantasize about the smell. I would pretend I had a cigarette in my hand, bring it to my lips, inhale deeply, then exhale and flick the imaginary ashes into the imaginary ashtray. It took a long time to let go of wanting a cigarette every time the phone rang or after a meal. I had dreams of smoking for years after I quit. And then, one day, I realized I didn't want a cigarette anymore. I was free!

Relapse

Well, not exactly. I relapsed. I was with someone who was smoking, and I asked if I could take a hit off the person's cigarette. That is part of cigarette etiquette, you know. If asked, you always offer a cigarette (unless it is your last one) or give a hit to someone. Sanitary considerations aside, I took lungful and immediately coughed. Two days later, I had bought a pack and was back to smoking.

I had failed. I was ashamed but secretly felt like I had gotten away with something. It took five attempts for me to actually, finally, totally, and permanently (for thirty-plus years now) quit.

Recommitment

From this experience, I learned some very important lessons. There is no shame in committing to change and not succeeding. Change takes effort to begin, sustain, and then maintain. As the song says, *"I get knocked down/ but I get up again/ You're never gonna keep me down."* (Chumbawamba, "Tubthumping") There is no guarantee that the change I wanted will last once I've achieved it, no matter how much I want things to be that way. I have to recommit to my new way of being every day.

We have to do the same thing with COVID-19. I am seeing people across the world making changes to how they live, work, play, and think about things. The effort needed to adapt to the requirements this pandemic has laid on us is huge. For me to remember to wash my hands, keep them away from my face, wear a mask when I am out in public, observe social distancing, and stay optimistic, while seemingly simple enough to do, is actually a complex and draining set of behavioral changes. No wonder people are pushing back. They just want a hit off that cigarette.

Of course, we know the danger of doing that. Here the tension is theatrical, with the audience (us) observing the unsuspecting hero or heroine walk into the trap laid (going to the beach, returning to work) by the dastardly villain (COVID-19). We can shout from the cheap seats, but the protagonist *must* make this error in judgment for the play to work itself out. Just as we must face the fact that people will refuse to wear a mask, will congregate on beaches and in restaurants. In spite of warnings, exhortations from medical professionals and caring politicians, there will be those who relapse.

Vulnerability

For those who are able to sustain recovery, a different set of challenges exists. There is the pull to revert to old ways of thinking and doing things. Vulnerability to relapse is high in the first few days, weeks, and months of recovery. Then, magically, a new way of being becomes the accepted standard. We no longer shake hands when greeting one another.

Everyone covers their mouth and nose in their elbow when sneezing. We no longer need measurements or marks on the ground to show us where to stand; six feet becomes the safe-distance cocoon we each occupy. And when this space is violated, we are aware and speak up.

This is actually one of the most vulnerable points in the change process because it marks the emergence of a certain mastery that can make one cocky. "I've got this COVID-19 thing licked!" you may think. Your unerring eye picks up the scofflaws who are not following the rules and puts them in some psychic jail for social misfits. Or maybe that's just me.

Stay the Course

On the other hand, there are those who never quite achieve mastery. For these souls, the tension between wanting things to be the way the used to be and coming to terms with the new state of affairs frequently causes them to withdraw and become anxious. For these folks, change never actually is achieved, and they remain caught between what used to be and what they fear might be.

I don't know how much longer I am going to have to be COVID-19-conscious. I am adopting new behaviors and trying to master them. I am paying attention to possible relapse should I forget my handwashing routine or not carry my mask with me everywhere I go.

I really want to take a hit off a cigarette, but I am going to continue to shelter in place and just focus on my recovery.

LEARNING NEW
BEHAVIORS

Originally published April 26, 2020

Was it just four months ago when this all started? Since January, I have acquired a whole new dictionary of acronyms: PPE, SARS, COVID-19, WHO, SIP. And I have increased my store of knowledge on virology, epidemiology, constitutional law, hospital staffing, and world distribution of supplies, including oil, toilet paper, and pork. I had no idea I would be taking a graduate course in twenty-first century economics, biology, and disease transmission.

I enrolled, unknowingly, in this course back in March. I thought I was taking a vacation. Instead, unknowingly, I became a test subject in a pandemic. I thought I was just traveling to Australia and New Zealand. Instead, unknowingly, I acquired a deadly virus. I thought I had allergies and lost my sense of smell (but just for a day). Instead, unknowingly, my body successfully dealt with COVID-19.

What has really happened in this time? From my vantage point, it seems that the things that I once thought were predictable and dependable aren't. It seems that, with enough reminding, I can keep my hands from my face. I can remember to wash tops and bottoms and in between my fingers. It seems I can drive with a mask. It seems I can relax more. It seems I can change my shopping habits and decrease the number of trips to the store. It seems I can learn new technology and get together with folks I know using video platforms. It seems I am sleeping better, exercising more, and only occasionally eating things that I shouldn't.

There is absolutely no way I could have predicted these things five months ago.

In such circumstances, entire populations are finding ways to change how they earn a living, interact, and get along with one another. For some, this is a welcome relief; for others, this is life and, sadly, death.

Disappointment

People are finding out that many institutions that appeared solid and predictable are made of sand. Accessing services and obtaining needed supplies, well-established distribution chains, unquestioned next-day delivery of whatever you ordered online, are all undergoing changes with impacts felt differently by different cohorts.

Those who either have poor access to technology or do not have the skills associated with it are left out altogether, finding stores empty and information limited to hearsay. Many older adults, even though they may have technology and skills, are experiencing a different kind of social distancing, as gathering spots such as senior centers, libraries, churches, and stores are either closed or limiting assembly.

Shock

Right now we are in a period of shock. The full impact of COVID-19 hasn't been felt. What typically happens after the shock wears off are moments of shame, anger, resentment, and looking for someone or something to blame. Some people get through this phase, find their footing, and start rebuilding. Others may experience deep grief over loss of people and pets, as well as loss of status and familiar routines. Frequently people turn to substances for relief. While doing so may help in the short term, the long-term consequences are often debilitating.

Certain populations will feel these emotions more keenly. Interestingly, as a group, older adults seem to be more resilient and, given adequate food, shelter, and access to health care, many older adults will weather this pandemic.

Elders are At Risk

There are elders who are particularly at risk, especially those who depend on food distribution from community resources, who are marginalized by language, color, and economic issues, and who may be targeted by scammers. While age alone does not increase vulnerability, poor health and chronic socioeconomic conditions do.

Not all who experience grief, loss, and distress will regain their footing. Some will need additional support for days, weeks, or months. Many of us will experience a sense of hopelessness and helplessness when faced with a longer return to "normal" than what we anticipated. Adapting to the new normal will take effort. There are effective strategies for navigating these waters.

Claiming Competency

Basically, there are five areas of focus that, if you attend to each daily, will provide you with a sense of competency as this pandemic unfolds: First, it is vital that we stay connected with each other. Loneliness and isolation negatively impact our immune systems. In COVID-19 times, it is important to stay connected to those who are supportive and perhaps to disconnect from those who are not. Ideally, we all have family and friends who are loving and supportive, but this may not always be the case.

Second, it is important to create a routine to follow so you can feel productive. Before COVID-19, many of us filled our days with work, volunteering, or both. This gave us structure and a sense of having accomplished something. The best way to achieve this sense of productivity while we shelter in place is having a daily routine. It will lower anxiety, improve sleep, and help to regulate the uncertainty that we are living with. Ideally, a daily routine will include some physical activity, some study, specific times for meals, and set times for getting up and going to bed. Weekly routines might include tasks such as laundry, cleaning, bathing, and shopping. Monthly routines might include paying bills.

Third, we need to nourish ourselves. The nourishment we need isn't limited to food! We can also nourish ourselves by helping each other. Among the many inspirational things that have come out of this pandemic are all the ways people are finding to make their communities better. Offering to shop for folks who can't get out, making masks, setting up get-togethers on social media, tutoring, organizing neighbors to go outside to sing (or howl), dressing up to take out the garbage are just some of the creative ways people are releasing their energy and nourishing themselves.

Fourth, it's essential to find those moments in the day where we can focus and calm that anxious interior voice that keeps asking "What if?" You can do so by having some structured activity during the day that stimulates your mind, calms your body, and allows you to release the tensions that build up. That activity might be something like listening to music, or reading an inspirational book, or doing yoga, Tai Chi, or other focused movement.

Finally, gratitude is finding and appreciating what is so. Right now, look around and find something of beauty that inspires you. Think of someone or something that has touched you deeply and allow that memory to fill you with good feelings. Express thanks and gratitude for having what you do have. These are valuable assets that will sustain you as we navigate the days ahead.

ABOUT THE AUTHOR

MARY L. FLETT, PHD is an author who used to be a psychologist. In addition to writing, she is a nationally-recognized speaker and has led seminars on aging across the country. In this third book in her series, *Aging with Finesse*, she shares her insights and wisdom gleaned from over 30 years of working with elders as a psychologist, and a lifetime of mentoring by older friends and relatives. She is the Executive Director of the Center for Aging and Values and, in her spare time, runs Five Pillars of Aging, offering online and in-person programs on how to age better and age well.

Made in the USA
Columbia, SC
07 December 2021